My Best Dog Days

My Previous Books:

Exposed to Winds
[Selected poems]

Construction Delay Claims
[Performance measurements]

Anecdotes of Would-be Experts
[Business experiences]

Thoughts in a Maze
[Various mysteries]

Trials and Errors
[Life experiences]

Characters
[A tribute to past friends]

Oddities
[False assumptions]

Connections
[Human beliefs & behaviors]

Conclusions Volumes I & II
[Reaching conclusions – right or wrong]

My Best Dog Days

Arthur O.R. Thormann

Specfab Industries Ltd.

Edmonton, Alberta

2012

Library and Archives Canada Cataloguing in Publication

Thormann, Arthur O. R. (Arthur Otto Rudolf), 1934-
    My Best Dog Days / Arthur O.R. Thormann.

ISBN 978-0-9916849-1-5

    1. Thormann, Arthur O. R. (Arthur Otto Rudolf), 1934-
I. Title.

PS8589.H54945Z466 2012   C813'.54   C2012-907887-5

Publisher: Specfab Industries Ltd.
                  13559 - 123A Avenue
                  Edmonton, Alberta, Canada
                  T5L 2Z1
                  Telephone: 780-454-6396

Publication assistance by

PAGEMASTER
PUBLISHING
PageMaster.ca

Cover Designs: Front: Photo of myself
                  Back: Love against Hate

I dedicate this book to my wife, Renate,
To my daughters, Nancy & Diana,
And to my grandchildren,
Garett, Megan, Samantha, and Jordan,
Who make my life worth living!
PS: I love you!

Again, my gratitude goes to my wife, Renate,
to my daughter Nancy, and to my friend
Pam Sigvaldason, for their valued advice.
All mistakes remaining are entirely mine.

Preface

Thus, every dog at last will have his day–
He who this morning smiled, at night may sorrow;
The grub today's a butterfly tomorrow.
Peter Pindar: *Odes of Condolence.*

It is not my intent to write an intensive autobiography. So far, my previous books contain a few, mainly work related, autobiographical sketches. In this book, I intend to fill in some gaps, which are mainly leisure related.

At first, I intended to write a book about my life with Renate, my wife. Later, I decided that this part of my life would leave out some important phases – like the events before I met Renate, and my time of contemplative thought processes – and I decided to include these phases.

Part I of the book starts with some momentous events of the year 1934, the year of my birth. Next, it covers a few salient events during my seventeen years in Germany, plus my first seven years in Canada.

Part II of the book covers my original plan. It describes my life with Renate, my children, and my grandchildren, as well as some close relatives and friends.

Part III of the book describes my contemplative life, when I delved into some puzzling questions. Although many of these questions are also the topics of my previous books, I felt it would be helpful to my readers if I included some aspects of this phase in this book.

Finally, let me explain to you how I chose the title for this book. Originally, I chose the title "My Life with Renate." Then, after deciding to add the other two phases, I changed the title to "My Life of Leisure." However, when I thought about this title, I decided it was not catchy enough, although accurate, and I came up with "My Best Dog Days." I could have called the book "My Best Heydays," but this would not have been accurate, because only a few of my leisure days were actually heydays.

Dog days are normally hot and humid days, but you can also define dog days as leisure days. The latter is sufficiently unknown to make the title catchy. Besides, the year of my birth was also the Chinese zodiac year of the dog. Knowing this, and if you prefer to believe in zodiacs, you could consider all my days dog days, the best of which are leisure days, of course – again, "My Best Dog Days."

Arthur O.R. Thormann
Edmonton, November 11, 2012

Contents

Part I:
My Instructive Years

The Momentous Year 1934

I was born in Berlin, Germany, on April 7, 1934, one day after my father's birthday, which my mother had aimed at; she missed it, because she had not consulted me – I wanted my own and not my father's birthday.

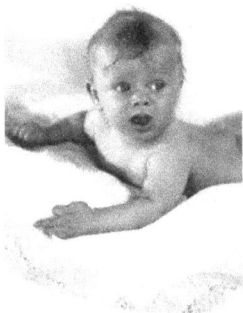

<<< Myself, shortly after I was born – looking astonished at my bewildering 1934 surroundings!

In any case, some particularly important events, other than my birth, made the year 1934 a very momentous year.

On the political scene, Germany and the Second Polish Republic signed the German-Polish ten-year Non-Aggression Pact on January 26, which must have pleased the Polish government. (However, it did not even last six years before Germany violated it.) As well, on February 9, Greece, Romania, Turkey, and Yugoslavia signed the Balkan Pact, and the Austrians had a civil war from February 12 to February 16.

On March 20, Heinrich Himmler, who was already Adolf Hitler's chief of the Gestapo (SS), took over all police forces in Germany, giving him vast power to abuse.

On June 30, the German Nazis purged Hitler's Sturmabteilung (SA), an act referred to as the "night of the long knives." On the same day, the SS took over the SA camp at Oranienburg. (Also of interest is that ten days later, on July 10, the SS killed German Social Democrat and author Erich Mühsam in Oranienburg's Concentration Camp, leaving no doubt about the aims and dangers of Germany's concentration camps.)

The May Constitution of 1934 had asserted the start of the Austro-fascist Federal State of Austria on May 1, and on July 25, Austrian Nazis assassinated Austrian's Chancellor Engelbert Dollfuss during a failed coup attempt.

On August 2, Adolf Hitler made sure he became the German Führer, i.e., the head of state as well as chancellor, and, six days later, the German Wehrmacht swore an oath of loyalty to him. Then, on August 19, in a quick referendum, ninety percent of the German population approved of Hitler's assumption of power.

On September 19, the Soviet Union joined the League of Nations. On October 16, the Long March of the Chinese Communists began. On December 27, Persia became Iran. Then, on December 29, Japan renounced both the Washington Naval Treaty of 1922 and the London Naval Treaty of 1930.

Those were the prominent events on the political scene. Across the Atlantic Ocean, Alcatraz became a prison on January 1. John Dillinger escaped from jail in Crown Point, Indiana, on March 3, using a wooden pistol. Ten days later, he and Baby Face Nelson with their gangs robbed the First National Bank in Mason City, Iowa. Then, on April 22, John Dillinger and two others shot their way out of an FBI ambush in northern Wisconsin. On May 15, the US Department of Justice offered a $25,000 reward for John Dillinger. Finally, on July 22, FBI agents outside Chicago's Biograph Theater mortally wounded Public Enemy #1, John Dillinger. (He might have been better off staying in the Crown Point jail.) On November 27, a gun battle with Baby Face Nelson, resulted in the death of one FBI agent, but mortally wounded special agent Samuel P. Cowley still killed Baby Face Nelson.

On the more general-interest scene, the producers released Frank Capra's movie *It Happened One Night* on February 22, starring Clark Gable, and Claudette Colbert. It was the first movie to win all five of the major Academy Awards.

As you can see, 1934 was a very decisive Year.

My Seventeen Years in Germany

I do not remember much before mid-1938, when my parents decided to take me along on a trip to Vienna. Vienna is a beautiful city situated on the Danube River in Austria. I can still vividly remember the beautiful buildings, the lively music, and the torte and cakes served in various Konditoreien – confectionery cafés.

My father also bought me a pair of lederhosen – leather shorts – with beautiful Austrian braces, and a little toy gun. I wore the lederhosen proudly when we returned to Berlin, to the envy of my friends.

Here, I proudly show off my new lederhosen, and my toy gun. Look carefully to see the slender wooden rod with the suction cup jutting from the barrel.

Another glowing memory I have of this period is my paternal grandfather, Otto Thormann, and his second wife, Helena, spending summer weekends in their garden-colony cottage at the outskirts of Berlin. They frequently invited us to join them for an afternoon, with Helena's delicious baked goods awaiting us.

Another salient event I remember of that period is when my father took me to the Hauptstrasse (the Main Street) in Schöneberg, our district in Berlin, where he expected the Führer, Adolf Hitler, to come along in his Mercedes open limousine. Crowds lined both sides of the street, and my father had to lift me to his shoulder to see anything. After about half an hour, the Führer's cabriolet did come along, and the crowds cheered deafeningly. Most people cried, "Sieg Heil," with their right arms fully extended. The Führer responded by raising his right forearm every few seconds.

Of course, I was in awe, with half a street-width separating us from the esteemed Führer of Germany. However, I must admit, his forbidding demeanor scared me a little. I began to have a tiny inkling of my mother and her friends' apprehensions about him – better not cross this man.

My mother moved in a circle of like-minded friends who criticized the Nazi regime. They were not Jews but Kaiser- and Hindenburg-regime supporters. However, they had to be careful to whom they relayed their criticisms: The careless ones usually ended up in concentration camps.

Then, war started. At first, the cruel effects of war eluded us. However, on August 25, 1940, just before I started school, British bombers hit Berlin. We were shocked. My father took me to a nearby street to view the damage. I still remember half an apartment building lying in ruins, and bathtubs dangling from the other half. My father looked sad. He said, "The Führer promised us this would never happen."

I was a happy student in my first school year. Then, my sisters and I developed a whooping cough, and the school prohibited my attendance until cured. Thankfully, my father personally tutored me to avoid my missing one school year, and my mother took us children to the sunny Baltic Sea island Usedom, to speed up the cure.

Once we were cured of the whooping cough, my father came along with me to my school and insisted on my reinstatement without loss of time. However, the principal was adamant that I must first pass some examinations. Gladly, I took and passed them.

My next memory is of the government drafting my father into the German army in February 1942. I felt sad. The stern tutoring my father had given me had somehow brought us closer.

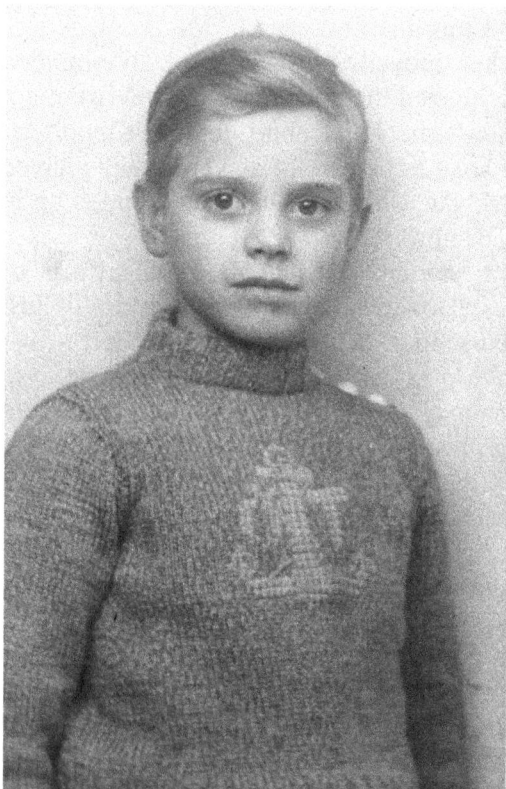

The sadness of losing my father, even temporarily, is evident here.

After he joined the army, I saw my father only a few short times during his leaves. I still remember him sending us a barrel full of herring from Norway, and bringing me a small bowie knife from Finland.

My next clear memory is of the serious bombings of Berlin during 1943. The government decided my evacuation turn had come; it sent me to foster parents near Posen, east of Berlin. My mother had just given birth to my youngest sister, Birgit, and the government ordered her to wait until she had recuperated.

During the following winter, I developed a frost boil on my right foot, which turned bluish from gangrene. My foster parents were scared and sent me off to join my mother; the government had evacuated her to a farmhouse in the village of Ponnsdorf, near the town of Finsterwalde. When I arrived, my mother immediately gave me a hot bath and scrubbed the boil until it bled. Within a week, it began to heal.

For the remainder of my fourth school year, I attended school in the small village of Ponnsdorf. The school accommodated about thirty children up to age fifteen, and one teacher taught all grades up to grade eight, all in the same room. This is where I met my first girlfriend, a blond girl named Christa Krüger.

However, our stay at Ponnsdorf did not last long. For some reason, my mother did not get along with the farmer in Ponnsdorf, and requested a transfer. The government found her other accommodations in a nearby village called Gröbitz. We occupied the entire second floor of a house at the edge of the village, on the road leading to Finsterwalde. My Aunt Anni and her two children joined us there as well.

One day, my mother sent my Cousin Renate and me to Finsterwalde to pick up some groceries. On our way home, Russian fighter planes directly attacked and nearly hit us, this was a new reality of war for us.

A few days later, we saw many Russian tanks rolling towards Berlin, and we had an intuition that the end of the war must be near. One Russian army unit based itself in Gröbitz, and we were very fortunate to receive enough food from the Russian soldiers to help us survive. Nevertheless, my mother decided to head back to Berlin.

So, one sunny morning in May 1945, we packed a few belongings and my three sisters onto a handcart, and started walking towards Berlin. On the first day, we got as far as Luckau, a town thirty kilometers north of Finsterwalde. We stayed overnight in a church hall filled with other refugees. The following day, we caught a freight train to Berlin.

Berlin was almost totally in ruins, including our apartment building. This did not faze my mother. She took us to her Aunt Ottilie's apartment, where we found the corpse of her great-aunt, whom she called Tante Pietsch. The neighbors told us that Aunt Ottilie had moved out to her cottage in a nearby garden colony, so we headed out there. Mother told her that Tante Pietsch had died, and that they should bury her as soon as possible, because of the unbearable stench she created in the apartment.

Aunt Ottilie was very helpful in many ways. She agreed to let us use her apartment, and provided us with the necessary food to survive long enough until we were able to fend on our own.

To receive food in Berlin after the war, we had to apply for ration cards. This was not a problem. The problem was getting fresh water. Corpses had badly contaminated most water sources in Berlin, except for the water out of the few ground pumps that existed. However, this source of water was barely enough for all users – one had to stand hours in line to receive it.

To make ends meet, I joined a gang of boys who stripped the ruins of salable or usable items, like metals and wood. The metals we sold to scrap dealers to get the money to buy food on the black market, and the wood we used, or sold to neighbors, for heating, to warm us during the cold winter months.

The war brought us other casualties as well. My father never returned to Berlin. He met, and fell in love with, a woman named Hilde, from Schleswig-Holstein. He divorced my mother to start a new life.

Hilde, and her daughter Lotti, with my father, Fritz, who holds one hand with her, and a cigar in his other hand

My mother, too, met a nice man named Hans Hammel – a WWII paratrooper.

Left to Right: My Sisters Karin & Waltraud, my Mother Angelika, my Sister Birgit, myself, and my Stepfather Hans Hammel

They eventually married, but did not live happily ever after. He came home one day with gonorrhea, and that ended the marriage. I had actually quite liked him, but I could not blame my mother for giving him the boot.

In 1949, I started an apprenticeship with Zeiss Ikon, as a precision instrument mechanic. However, near the end of two years of my apprenticeship, my mother decided to emigrate to Canada, to join her parents. The management of Zeiss Ikon was unhappy to lose me, but eventually agreed to give me a release.

Our ship, *SS Gripsholm* of the Swedish American Line, sailed from Bremerhafen at the end of March 1951. We arrived in Halifax, Canada, on April 8, one day after my seventeenth birthday.

My First Seven Years in Canada

After arriving in Halifax, we boarded a train for Edmonton, Alberta, where my mother's Brother Albert picked us up and drove us to my grandparents' farm, three miles north of Barrhead. My mother's long-awaited reunion with her parents was both joyful and tearful. We spent the remainder of the day talking about various miseries we had experienced during the war and postwar years.

Next day, my Grandfather Reinhold Jeske slaughtered two pigs – he expected to feed a starved family for a while.

The following week, my grandfather enrolled me in Barrhead's high school. Although I had not yet had any high-school education, the schoolteachers, after talking to me, started me out in grade eleven, but even this grade did not challenge me.

When not in school, I helped my grandfather with his farm chores. In July, we were clearing brush on his land, and I impaled a rotten root in my right shinbone. My grandfather pulled it out with a pair of pliers and poured Lysol into the wound. The wound healed in a few days, but I could hardly walk on the leg. We had it X-rayed, but the X-ray showed nothing but a swelling.

In August, I heard of a Swiss herbalist. People claimed he worked wonders. I slowly walked, with the help of a stick, the mile to see him. He asked me to stay with him for a few days. He suspected a lingering infection and applied an herbal plaster to extract it. After three days, puss began to drain. Two days later,

Old Doc,[1] as people called him, put Ozonol cream on the wound to heal it faster.[2]

I stayed with Old Doc for the remainder of the year, to help him gather herbs, and chop firewood for cooking and heating. In addition, I helped a nearby farmer stook his sheaves of grain. During this time, I also helped a chap named Ted Morris in Barrhead, who fixed farmers' tractors for Westlock's Doherty's Garage. Ted Morris, impressed with my mechanical ability, found me a job with Jimmy Dawson, his friend who owned Edmonton Auto Parts in Edmonton.

I started with Edmonton Auto Parts in January 1952. At first, I stayed at my Uncle Rudi's house, paying him the going rate for room and board, but when he complained that I ate too much, I moved out and found a room downtown.

I met a chap named Siegfried Friedrich. He called himself Fred, and worked as a welder in a downtown machine shop. We became friends and rented a room together to save on expenses.

In early 1953, we both quit our jobs and started working with Bill Bleiler. Bill had an idea to teach using the slide rule, which was still popular at the time. I knew slide rules used logarithmic graduations, and offered to graduate a five-foot wooden slide rule for Bill, which he intended to use to teach slide-rule techniques to students. Bill was glad to accept my offer, and paid me a modest fee.

---

[1] Old Doc's name was Alphonse Pfiffner, and he had no doctors' degree.

[2] However, eight months later, I needed an operation to scrape the infection from the shinbone.

Unfortunately, Fred and I did not earn enough during the next two months to pay for lodgings and food, and we wanted to leave for greener pastures. We decided to hitchhike to South America, and packed our few belongings into two overseas trunks. We shipped these trunks via rail to an eastern Canadian port city, and intended to follow hitchhiking across Canada. Once in the port city, we planned to seek employment on some ship sailing to South America.

No sooner had we shipped the trunks, we had second thoughts and changed our minds. We decided Canada offered more opportunities for us, and went to the railroad station to retrieve our trunks. However, the trunks had already left Edmonton, and we had to wait two weeks to get them back, at additional cost.

By this time, we were already living on borrowed money, and we decided to sign up for jobs with Eldorado Mining and Refining Limited, a uranium mining company in Northern Saskatchewan, which operated the Beaverlodge Mine near Uranium City. The company offered two jobs: one in its laundry, and one in its mill. Fred took the one in the laundry, and I took the one in the mill – as third-class mill mechanic.

We also signed up for a correspondence course on radio technology. We were hoping this course would ensure us better work.

At the Beaverlodge Mine, neither Fred nor I particularly liked our jobs, but, through overtime, we were able to earn a good income. We saw and learned a lot. We saw men foolishly losing their hard-earned money gambling. We saw normally intelligent men becoming absurd after drinking alcohol. We saw sex-crazed men fighting for the favors of an Indian prostitute. We learned how the Mine Mill and Smelters Union dealt with its dissidents. We learned that one should not row a canoe *across* the lake. Furthermore, I saw first-hand that electricians were the elite among the workers: well paid, and less taxing work. Yes, we saw and learned a lot.

After three months of working in the refining mill, I developed chest pains, and my foreman advised me to take a break (in case uranium radiation should be the cause). Fred, who, by then, had had enough of his job in the laundry, suggested we quit.

We returned to Edmonton in early August 1953. We rented our previous accommodation, and paid our debts. Then, we decided to become electricians and go job hunting. We looked up the addresses of some electrical contractors and set out for interviews. The first one, Johnson Brothers Electrical Contracting, turned us down. The superintendent told us they did not intend to hire new apprentices for a while. We got the same response at Industrial Power. Next, we went to Birmingham Electric. Mr. Birmingham, the owner himself, interviewed us, and said he could only hire one new apprentice at that time. He looked at me and said, "You can start Monday morning." We thanked him and left. Then, we stopped in at Progress Electric. Again, the owner himself, Mr. Webb, interviewed us. When we told him we had taken a radio technology correspondence course, he was impressed and asked us some questions involving electrical formulas. Math was one of my fortes, and I answered his questions without hesitation. He, too, said he could only hire one new apprentice, and told me to report for work on Monday morning. It was already late afternoon, and neither Fred nor I felt like going for another interview. We decided to stop at a beer parlor for refreshments.

Fred looked disappointed and said, "What next?"

I said, "Well, Fred, we have two jobs to fill."

"Yes," said Fred, "but only one employee."

"Not necessarily," I replied.

"What do you mean? You're the one hired at both places."

"That's true," I said, "but I have the feeling that Mr. Birmingham is a late-morning starter. Why don't you report for work at Birmingham Electric on Monday and tell whoever is in charge that you are the new apprentice Mr. Birmingham hired?"

"Do you think they'll be fooled by that?"

"It's worth a try," I said.

Thus, on Monday, we both reported for work. Fred reported at Birmingham Electric, and I reported at Progress Electric. Neither of the owners was there to welcome us.

The respective supervisors of each company gave both of us assignments that required driving a half-ton truck. Three months later, within the same week, as it happened, both of us had a driving accident. Back at the shop, Walter Kirmse, my supervisor, told me to report to Mr. Webb.

I went to Mr. Webb's office and reported to him that I had stopped at an intersection when a truck in front of me pulled away. I had a quick look left and right and pulled away. Not realizing that the truck in front of me had suddenly stopped, I drove right under one of his protruding beams and dented the hood.

Mr. Webb nodded, got up, and went to the yard to inspect the damage. He told Walter Kirmse to order a new hood. Then he turned to me and said, "You better get going to complete your assignments."

I was stunned. "You want me to continue driving the truck?" I asked him.

"How else are you going to complete your jobs?" He wanted to know.

"I just thought…the accident…" I stammered.

"You've learned your lesson, haven't you?"

"Well, yes."

"Then get going!"

Fred, too, had to report his accident to his boss, Mr. Birmingham. Mr. Birmingham took one good look at Fred and said, "You're not the one I hired."

Fred said, "But I have worked here for the past three months."

Mr. Birmingham shook his head and listened to Fred's accident report. Then, he inspected the damage and told Fred to report for work at some west-end job site, and he told the supervisor, "Don't give any more truck-driving assignments to Fred."

Fred and I had quite a chuckle at our respective bosses' different reactions to our accidents. However, Fred was glad that Mr. Birmingham did not fire him.

At Progress Electric, I met another apprentice named Gottlieb Hoffmann. He called himself Gus. It did not take us long to become friends. We also managed to attend Calgary's technical school together a few times.

The school sessions lasted two months in each of the first three years, and three months in the last year of our apprenticeship. After we completed the last session of technical school, Gus and I decided to take a six-week vacation and explore the "Wild West."

We left Edmonton on July 2, 1957, and drove to Montana, where a car accident delayed us a day. After two days in Great Falls, we drove to the Yellowstone National Park in Wyoming, and from there to Idaho Falls. Next, we drove to Salt Lake City, Utah, where we spent three days. Then, we continued to Arizona and the Grand Canyon. Next, to Boulder City, Nevada, the Hoover Dam, one day in Las Vegas, then on to Blythe, Palm Springs, and Baldwin Park, where Gordon and Kay Michie had their house.

<<< *Our good friends, Kay & Gordon Michie*

The Michies were out, so we continued to Los Angeles, and went swimming at Santa Monika Beach. In the evening, we returned to Baldwin Park. Gordon invited us to stay for a few days.

19

We went sunbathing to some beaches, shopping in Los Angeles, photographing in Hollywood, and roaming at Disneyland.

One day, we went to Long Beach, where the sixth Miss Universe Pageant was held. We pretended to be media photographers, and the various contestants did not mind posing for us. We especially liked Miss Canada.

<<< Gloria Noakes, Miss Canada 1957

She was a very beautiful and friendly woman. We introduced ourselves, and told her we were from Alberta, Canada, on a tour of America's Wild West. Then, we assured her that if it were up to us she would be the next Miss Universe. She thanked us, and gave us a big smile.[3]

---

[3] However, Gladys Zender of Peru ended up as Miss Universe 1957, and Gloria Noakes made eighth runner-up.

Next, we went for a day to Mexico; Gordon joined us. However, it took Gordon and me an hour to convince the custom officials to let us back into the United States, because the USA had granted Bessarabia-born Gus only a single-entry visa.

After parting with the Michies, we drove north, to Monterey, and then to San Francisco, where we stayed four days, thoroughly enjoying ourselves. Then, we headed further north, to Eureka first, next to Portland, Oregon, and on, for a day, to Seattle, Washington.

Right after leaving San Francisco, the weather had turned misty and foggy, and this condition followed us to Vancouver, Canada, where we met up with Fred, who had decided to leave Alberta. We spent almost three days sightseeing with Fred. I think this was the last time we spent time together as bachelors.

Gus, Fred, and myself, with Vancouver in the background

After leaving Vancouver, we stopped briefly at Kimberly, BC, then, continued on to sunny Alberta. We spent two days in Calgary, visiting with Hans and Helga Hohenwarter. On August 12, 1957, we arrived back in Edmonton, where our girlfriends, Renate and Inge, had anxiously awaited our return.

During my next major event, in November 1957, I gladly became a Canadian citizen.

In addition, on my return to work at Progress Electric, Vic Webb offered me the estimator's job – a turning point for me, which opened new vistas.

Due to the closer proximity of our new working relationship, Vic Webb and his wife Myrtle started to influence my spiritual life. They would frequently invite me to join them for lunch, and Vic Webb would start out with a short prayer, or by reading an excerpt from the Book of Psalms.

Vic Webb took the Bible literally. Although I had a passable knowledge of Martin Luther's translation of the Bible, he was a virtual walking encyclopedia of the Authorized (King James) Version, and when I pointed out some serious discrepancies in the translations, he became disturbed and started his own translations from original Greek versions. As well, I questioned some of God's actions, as related in the Book of Genesis. This really got him shook up. As I said, he took the Bible literally.[4]

I must say, a more pleasant experience was my time spent with Renate Sowa, my new girlfriend, who became a major influence in my life.

---

[4] I have listed a few of these discrepancies and questionable actions by God in some of my previous books.

Renate (1957) is the woman with whom I fell in love, and to whom I proposed marriage.

She accepted, and we lived happily ever after.

In all these years, Renate never lost her high principles, her inner beauty, and her exceptional grace.

She is strong-willed, frugal, conscientious, curious, courageous, and tolerant. She likes gardening, cooking, baking, and sewing.

She is quite a woman!

I first met Renate at her older Sister Sigrid's[5] New Year's Eve party in 1956. Renate and her younger Sister Inge had just arrived in Canada from Germany a few weeks earlier.

Since I was the proud owner of a car at that time, I frequently picked Renate up from work and drove her home. On the way home, we used to stop at a coffee shop for a chat. It must have been obvious to people around us that we were in love. I courted Renate for about sixteen months.

---

[5] Sigrid nicknamed herself Sigi, and pronounced it Siggi.

Renate on the hill near Jasper, where I gave her the engagement ring

Then, I invited her to climb a big hill with me near Jasper, where, kneeling, I proposed marriage to her. She accepted, and I gave her an engagement ring. We were both elated.

We set our wedding day for November 29, 1958, and Sigi volunteered to make all the arrangements.

Sigi was like a fourth sister to me. She called me Brüderchen, the German diminutive for brother, and I called her Schwesterchen, the German diminutive for sister. We never lost our affection for each other.

Renate and I had our marriage ceremony in Sigi's Lutheran church, and our wedding spread in the basement of Sigi's house. Sigi borrowed the required chairs for the guests from her church, had the men set up a table of two 4x8-plywood sheets, and covered them with her best linen tablecloths.

Renate and I on our wedding day, November 29, 1958

She loaded the table with all her self-prepared exotic dishes, plus a homemade punch consisting of white wine, ginger ale, and various fruits. Sigi was quite an organizer, and we could not thank her enough.

Our wedding guests consisted mostly of my friends and relatives. From Renate's side, only her Sisters Sigi and Inge were present. None of her three other sisters nor her parents could make it.

Part II:
My Constructive Years

First Years of Marriage

Our first year of marriage was hectic, to say the least. We moved into a one-bedroom apartment and spent all of our savings furnishing it.

Then, two-and-a-half months before the end of our second year of marriage, I invited Renate out to a special dinner. We were just heading into a most beautiful Indian summer.

"What's the occasion?" she wanted to know.

"I want to discuss our future with you," I replied.

Renate had a good job as a lab technician at the Royal Alexander Hospital, and Vic Webb, my boss, had just promoted me to be the assistant manager at Progress Electric.

After dinner, as we relaxed with a glass of liqueur and a cup of coffee, Renate enquired, "What do you wish to discuss about our future?"

I said, "Don't you think it's about time to start a family?"

She seemed stunned for a moment. Then, she said, "I would have to give up my job for a while."

I shrugged and said, "Maybe for a long time. I think children need to be looked after properly for a few years, at least until they start school."

"Can we afford this?" she asked.

"I think so. Vic Webb increased my salary as assistant manager. Besides, we'll probably get some income from our investments."

She was silent for a few minutes. I could sense

the wheels turning in her mind. Then, she said, "Well, let's go home and start our family."

I just smiled at her and said, "Remind me if I'm speeding, driving home."

She laughed and said, "I will!"

<<< Myself with Nancy & Renate

A little over nine months later, Renate gave birth to our cute little daughter Nancy. We stayed in our one-bedroom apartment for another eight months, and then, in March 1962, we bought a three-bedroom house (with a garden!) in Edmonton's Dovercourt district. Renate was happy that she finally had a garden, and Nancy got her own bedroom.

In April 1964, Renate gave birth to our second cute daughter, Diana, who received the third bedroom.

Our two daughters could not have had a better tutor than Renate. Renate was a good grammarian of the German language, and taught it to both girls, in addition to English, of course.

By the time the girls started school, they were truly bilingual. Renate also taught them gardening, cooking, preserving the various fruits and vegetables from the garden, and sewing their own dresses. In addition, we liked traveling, which gave our girls an even broader outlook.

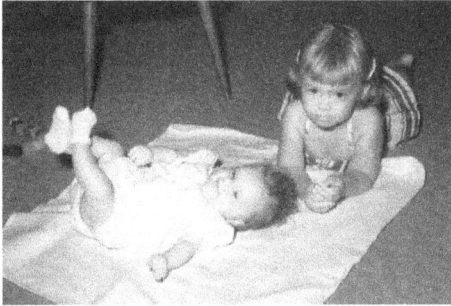

<<< Nancy and Diana – Nancy looks rather sad, probably because she lost some of mom's attention

In 1966, Renate's parents decided to pay us a visit. They came to us for Christmas and New Year's Eve. Early in 1967, they decided to escape our Canadian winter and visit Sigi, who had moved to San Jose, California. We agreed to pick them up in San Jose during May, and drive them back to Canada.

Our 1967 Trip to California

Come May, we started packing our things for the trip. We decided to take our camping equipment along, to introduce our girls to outdoor life.

At the end of the first day of travel, we pitched our tent at a campsite along the Columbia River – a mistake, as it turned out. The wind along the river was so strong that the tent kept flapping all night. I was seriously concerned that the tent stakes might pull out of the ground. We got very little sleep that night.

At sunrise, half frozen, we packed up and headed for the nearest coffee shop to restore our energy. The girls asked for pancakes and orange juice, and Renate and I opted for bacon, eggs, hash browns, and a strong cup of coffee.

"Let's relax in a motel tonight," Renate pleaded.

"That's for sure!" I promised her.

In the afternoon of the third day, we arrived safely at Sigi's house in San Jose. As I opened the car door and stepped out, Sigi came running out of the house and hugged me with shining eyes.

"How is my Brüderchen?" she cried.

"Fine, Schwesterchen," I answered.

Celebrations started already the first evening, when Sigi introduced us to some of her neighbors. Sigi had prepared for us a small table full of hors d'oeuvres. My Brother-in-law Klaus, Sigi's husband, served us some excellent California wines, and Sigi promised to take us on a wine-tasting tour before driving home.

Klaus's Cousin Horst, and his wife Maudi, also came for a visit, and promised to join us on a shopping tour in San Francisco the next day. Of course, we ended up in Chinatown, not my father-in-law's favorite place, as it turned out. He particularly disliked the Chinese food, and we promised to take him for western food in the future.

My father-in-law was very humorous, though. He had amusing stories for every occasion. Even setbacks like Chinese food evoked some humor from him.

The wine-tasting tour was more to his liking, and he purchased a few bottles of the best for us, plus a couple of jars of excellent vineyard pesto for our evenings' hors d'oeuvres.

The weather was warm for May, and Sigi took us a few times to some beaches, for relaxing and tanning. Klaus, on the other hand, took us ocean fishing for salmon one day. The catch was negligible, but we had a lot of fun trying.

We also visited the California Mystery Spot, near Santa Cruz. The brochure told us of a gravity-defying force that even mystified the famed physicist Albert Einstein. My in-laws were visibly awed, walking up a wall in a room of a building, and as my father-in-law, who was a few inches shorter, attained my height standing opposite me on a concrete platform.[1]

We had a lot of fun with our relatives, but our vacation days were rapidly dwindling. Leave-taking from Klaus and Sigi was our only sad experience on this trip, and we had to promise them to come again for a visit as soon as possible.

"Take care of yourself, Brüderchen," said Sigi, tearfully.

"You, too, Schwesterchen," I replied, and gave her a big hug.

On the way back, we took the coastal highway and stopped at a few more points of interest, like the famous trees of mystery, and the sea lion caves.

---

[1] I found out later that the landowners of these mystery spots create these effects by distorting the architecture and landscape, to give slanted visitors the illusion everything around them is level.

Klondike Days in Edmonton

Klondike Days was a ten-day annual exhibition and fair held during the last days of July, originally known as the "Edmonton Exhibition." In 1964, organizers chose the new theme on the premise that Edmonton was the stopover for prospectors on the way to the Yukon Territory during the Klondike Gold Rush.

The people of Edmonton and their visitors embraced the new theme with delight, dressing up in the former period's costumes.

Our family was no exception. When we returned from California, Renate and Inge right away started on a big sewing project, using old publications of former costumes as their guides.

Both women were busy for about three weeks, sewing, and fitting, old-timer outfits for us, and for their parents. They were finally satisfied we would all pass for old-timers. However, this sewing activity did not stop us from celebrating birthdays, going on picnics, and going on camping and fishing trips.

Most people who had decided to dress up in old-timer outfits were showing off along Jasper Avenue on weekends during Klondike Days, while just as many killjoys were busy photographing them.

In addition, the exhibition at Northlands Park offered an interesting fair, with knickknack, hotdog, and hamburger stands, as well as arts displays. We spent our evenings rehashing each day's events, and planning for more enjoyment the next day, but ten days gave us hardly enough time to enjoy everything, especially trying to satisfy the curiosity of our children and their grandparents. Nevertheless, we had just as much fun planning our actions as we had taking them.

<<< The Thormann Klondikers, all of us in outfits sewn by Renate

A few gambling stands at Northlands Park also offered us opportunities to lose some money, rolling big wooden dice, and so on. The women were not too interested in these, but Gus and I, and our father-in-law, huddled together to discuss our ideas regarding how we might beat the odds against us. Then, we tried our luck at the various games – without much success, I must admit.

More Visits & Trips

Renate's Sister Margret and her husband Werner came to visit us in 1969. We took them to various places of interest in Alberta, but the event I remember most vividly is Neil Armstrong's landing on the Moon[2] in July 1969, while they were with us. Werner was so excited that he bought a map of the moon to pinpoint the exact landing site. We spent literally hours watching various TV reports and looking at this map.

---

[2] Neil Armstrong was the mission commander of the *Apollo 11* Moon landing in July 1969. Buzz Aldrin was with him in the *Eagle*, the lunar module (LM) while Michael Collins remained in *Columbia*, the Command & Service Module (CM). Before landing on the Moon, Armstrong noticed that they were heading towards an unsafe landing area, and took over manual control of the LM. However, this search used up valuable fuel for propellant liftoff after landing and extra-vehicular-activity (EVA). After Armstrong confirmed touchdown, Houston expressed its worries as "You got a bunch of guys about to turn blue. We're breathing again." Almost five hours after touchdown, Neil Armstrong set foot on the lunar surface, with the famous words, "That's one small step for [a] man, one giant leap for mankind." About twenty minutes later, Aldrin joined Armstrong as the second man to set foot on the Moon, and the two men started their two-and-a-half-hour EVA. Shortly after they planted the flag of the United States of America on the Moon, President Richard Nixon congratulated them by telephone from his office. He spoke to them for about one minute, and Armstrong responded for thirty seconds. After helping Aldrin setting up the Early Apollo Scientific Experiment Package, Armstrong went for a sixty-five-yard walk to East Crater, the longest distance traveled from the LM on this mission. Armstrong and Aldrin had a successful Moon liftoff, docked with the CM, and the three astronauts returned to Earth.

Werner and I were awed, of course, but my Uncle Rudi, a devout Pentecostal Church member, gave us his assertion that all was just a big hoax.

My father's stepdaughter, Lotti, notified me in June 1971 that my father had died on May 26, at age 61. May 15, he had collapsed with a hemorrhage caused by a duodenal ulcer, and they rushed him to a hospital. His doctors performed an operation on him May 17, but his heart failed him nine days later.

Renate and I had planned a trip to Germany for the following year, and, when I received this sad news, I wished we had decided to make the trip earlier.

However, we did accept Sigi's invitation in 1971 to visit them and admire their new swimming pool.

Here, I am showing off my dive into Klaus & Sigi's new swimming pool, with Nancy & Diana in the background.

We adhered to our plan the following year and visited Renate's parents for Christmas. We stayed at their house in Borken, and we were fortunate to meet most of Renate's relatives there, who came to visit us.

My Cousin Wolfgang and his wife, Ingelore, paid us a visit, too. His father, i.e., my father's brother, had died in June that year, also age 61. Even though we had a sadness to share, we were happy to get together again after nearly thirty years of separation.

I also wanted to meet up again with some of my relatives and friends in Berlin. So, after New Year's Day, 1973, I made a quick trip to the city of my birth. I stayed at my Aunt Anni's apartment, the aunt who had joined us with her two children in Gröbitz. Her doctors had just diagnosed her with cancer, and had prescribed Devil's Claw tea for her to drink. I had never heard of Devil's Claw tea, and she gave me a package of it to take back to Canada.

Klaus Frese, a teenage friend of mine during my after-war years in Berlin, showed me some of the reconstruction in Berlin since I had left, including the Berlin Wall.[3] We had heard about this wall in Canada, of course, but in reality, it looked more ominous than I had imagined. In fact, I could not believe what I saw, with all the watchtowers manned by East Germans with submachine guns. Was this the land of Frederick the Great, Goethe, and Schiller, or did I accidentally

---

[3] The Berlin Wall was a barrier constructed in 1961-62 by the German Democratic Republic (East Germany) to protect its population from so-called "fascist" elements in West Berlin and West Germany. In practice, the barrier prevented massive emigration and defection from the East German Communist Bloc.

end up in a land of earlier-century barbarians?

Most of the Berliners I met on this trip looked sick to me. Perhaps this was because of the overcast winter weather in January 1973, but I believe most Berliners were sick, if not physically, then in spirit. The only one who appeared normal to me was my Cousin Uwe, Aunt Anni's son. He owned a decoration business, and was quite an artist. He gave me a few of his carvings to take back to Canada, which, for the most part, I delivered to his father, my Uncle Alex.

Back in Borken, it was time for us to say our farewells to Renate's parents. The one I would miss the most was my father-in-law, Tony Sowa. He was truly a one-of in my life. The last time I saw him was in 1981, when we made another trip to Germany to attend his 50th Wedding Anniversary. Although this was supposed to be a happy occasion, and it was for the most part, he had not seemed happy to me. When he and I went for a walk together, he hinted that his end was near. "I have lived a full life," he assured me. Eighteen months later, we received the sad news of his death.

<<< Tony Sowa and I, toasting each other farewell.

I had to make a few trips to attend trustees' educational conferences, but for our family vacation trips, Renate and I chose the Hawaiian Islands, and the Okanagan Valley and Victoria in British Columbia.

Our Sports & Games

Our main active sports consisted of hunting, fishing, camping, bowling, swimming, skating, skiing, and some tennis. Renate also became an excellent curler. Our main spectator sport was Canadian football. The sport captivated us so much that we even listed to it on radio broadcasts during our hunting and fishing trips. Most of our fishing trips involved lake and river fishing, but we also went on a few ocean-fishing trips.

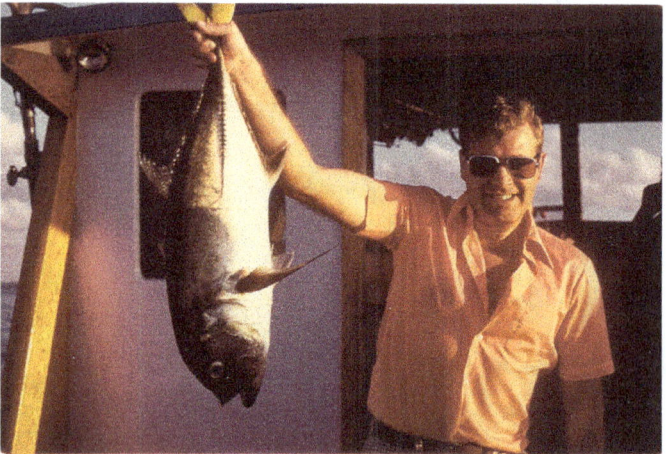

I'm proudly holding up my catch off the coast of the Bermuda Islands.

I eventually gave up hunting when I lost my good hunting partner Rudi Hoffmann. Rudi had a stroke in his early fifties and died a few days later. Hunting no longer appealed to me after that.

These sports took up a great deal of our time, but we also found the time to play games.

One game we played a lot is Stock Ticker. We liked it because it resembled our investment decisions. Another game we liked to play is Skat. This is a German card game equivalent to the English card game Bridge. I also played some Bridge, but I found Skat more challenging. We also played most of the other popular games, like Scrabble, Checkers, and Chess. Vic Webb loved playing Chess. At this game, he and I won equally often – perhaps I won one or two more games than he did. He also liked to play pool.

Vic and I playing eight ball

We played mostly eight ball or snooker games. At these games, he was the better player, since he practiced a lot on his own pool table at home (above).

Aiming at a Higher Education

I was never fortunate enough to get a university education, other than some courses in mechanical engineering and investment strategies. When I came to Canada, at a time in my life when I should have attended university, I was too busy trying to make ends meet. Later, when I could have afforded to attend university, I was too busy building a family life.

I missed attending university, of course, but I tried to make up for it by reading books. Nevertheless, books cannot completely take the place of university, which also teaches students to think for themselves. Having come to this conclusion, I decided to make a higher education possible for our daughters, and, eventually, for our grandchildren. Our daughters took advantage of this, and ended up with university degrees. I sincerely hope that our grandchildren will take advantage of this as well. Megan has already done so, getting herself a commerce degree in 2011, at age 20. This enabled her to get an excellent job offer from the Telus Corporation.

Garett, so far, is getting his higher education from books, as I do, and from the internet, as I do. At this point, I must say something in favor of the internet. Sure, one can go to the library, and, with some luck, find a book that has the information one seeks to find, but this is very time-consuming. On the internet, one enters a word, or a phrase, and bingo! One gets a multitude of places where one can find the information one seeks.

This is why our youngsters love the internet. Still, for a decent job in our civilization, one still needs a university degree.

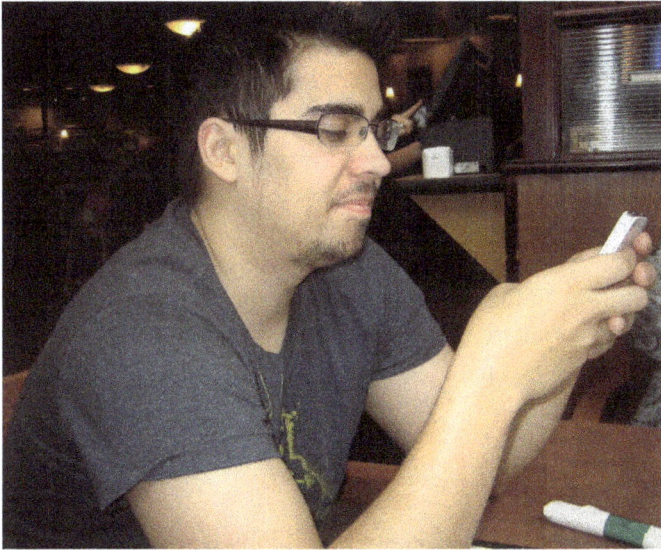

Garett, looking up important information on his iPhone

On the other hand, a degree does not guarantee university graduates a job, but without such a degree, landing a job that requires a higher education becomes almost impossible. This lack of guarantee is often a deterrent to spend several years at university, but an education must also serve a nobler purpose than getting a better job, namely, to aid the advancement of human civilization. Each generation must pass its educational advancements on to the next generation. If one cannot find another purpose in life, this purpose should suffice.

Even before human beings started to record their history in writing, they passed on their accumulated knowledge from generation to generation. They did this orally and through practical demonstrations. After human beings started recording their history in writing, approximately 3500 B.C., educators passed their knowledge on to students more rapidly, and this transfer of knowledge accelerated over the centuries. However, in earlier times, only a few people received a higher education. In some cases, scribes made their knowledge, like the hieroglyph system, purposely more difficult to learn to preserve their status. Today, a higher education is easily available to all who can afford it, and our youngsters should aspire to take advantage of it.

Part III:
My Contemplative Years

Why Contemplate?

We usually contemplate when something puzzles us. I have contemplated a lot in my life, because a lot has puzzled me. For example, what gets life started? This may not seem like a puzzle, but, unbelievably, it still puzzles our scientists, therefore, I am in good company.

Here are some more examples: Does life have meaning or purpose? If so, what is it? Does God exist? If so, does He – assuming God is a male – have partial (human) traits, or is He neutral and impartial? In addition, if God exists, is Satan necessary to satisfy the world's duality principles? Then, does the soul exist? If so, what constitutes the soul? Is it immortal? Does it return to Earth? Do animals have souls, too? If not, what makes humans so special? etc. These are a few basic puzzles without good answers.

Philosophers, too, contemplate a lot, but I think they try too hard to find answers where answers may not exist. In the final analysis, the above puzzles may stem mainly from our vanity. It is always easy to convince ourselves that we exist to serve a special purpose, here on Earth as well as for a future life.

Furthermore, we have problems believing that our bodies are the product of natural selection. It is more plausible to us that our bodies are the product of someone's, perhaps God's, creative design, and we have no problems applying similar "logical" thinking to our entire universe. The belief that everything grew and developed from chaos seems illogical to us.

Most thinking people engage in these sorts of contemplations, I am sure, but this still does not answer the question, why contemplate? To put it simply, I believe we contemplate to satisfy our vain curiosities, even if we do not find satisfactory answers.

Presumptions versus Facts

During my years of contemplation, presumptions that assume a factual character particularly disturbed me. For example, you may ask someone, even a total stranger, "Do you believe in God?" If the person of whom you asked this question chooses to respond, the responses could be "yes," "no," or "I don't know," and when you get a "yes" or "no" answer, you may ask this follow-up question: "What supports your belief?" Now, if the responder chooses to reply to this question, and his/her answer to the previous question was "yes," he or she might give you these sorts of explanation:

1. "I believe the Bible's assertions about God." or
2. "God speaks to me occasionally." or
3. "God answers my prayers." or
4. "I look at the marvelous designs around us, and I believe that such designs can only have been created by a Superior Being like God."

On the other hand, if the responder's answer to the previous question was "no," he or she might give you these sorts of explanation:

5. "I just do not believe that God, if he exists, would allow the miseries to occur that befall us." or

6. "I do not believe in anything I cannot see, feel, or touch." or

7. "I have a problem with the Bible's assertions about God." or

8. "I have never had a single response from God to my requests." or

9. "The concept of God is too unscientific for me to believe."

All of these responses are presumptuous, even response #8. Although what happened to responder #8 may be factual, his or her conclusion about the existence of God is presumptuous, because God may simply have chosen not to respond to him or her.

Our problem is, we assume the existence or nonexistence of an entity like God, or Satan, or the soul, or ghosts, and then, instead of looking for facts to support our assumption, we use presumptions for support. The key to successful support in such cases is, search for the facts rather than using presumptions.

Noticeable Transformations

At the start of the 1970s, I had the distinct feeling that we were heading into a period of transformation – not just individual but collective transformation. After all, we had just witnessed Neil Armstrong's moon landing in July 1969, which opened new vistas for us, indeed.

Our youngest daughter, Diana, started school in 1970 – an additional transformation for her – which also provided Renate with a transformation, namely, to devote more time to her favorite hobbies, like painting, gardening, and sewing.

My own life began to change more drastically. At Progress Electric, Vic Webb had promoted me to manager, which attached even more responsibility to my already onerous work. I was also president of the Edmonton Chapter of the Electrical Contractors Association of Alberta, and, as such, automatically a director of the parent association and the association's board of directors asked me to chair the Business and Public Relations Committee. In addition, I started to teach the association's electrical estimating course.

Then, barely a year later, the board of directors appointed me as one of management's two trustees on a joint trust fund with the union for a newly negotiated health and welfare plan. This trusteeship became a major force of transformation in my life. In addition to the work required to design and set up the plan, my trustee's responsibilities were akin to the difficult task I had once performed as a juror.

My spiritual life underwent a transformation, too. After surviving an explosion in an electrical manhole, which left me blinded for more than two weeks, the quests for life's meaning and purpose entered my mind. In fact, my first poem dealt with this search. The lines and verses of the poem came to me rather quickly, and, blinded by the explosion, I had to dictate the poem to Renate. My poetic side remained with me circa twenty years; then disappeared as fast as it came.

At the same time, books written by Albert Schweitzer, who advocated the reverence for life, finally convinced me to give up hunting. However, I had already developed distaste for hunting.

There were other transformations as well: The younger generation favored promiscuity; homosexuals demanded the same rights as society granted heterosexuals; Doctor Henry Morgentaler decided to challenge the law regarding abortions; and ordinary people were heading into the computer age, including myself.

Computers immediately impressed me. I had visions of vast vistas opening up for us with the aid of computers. Vic Webb and I flew to Denver, Colorado, for a week, to take a computer course. The instructors taught us computer basics and simple program designs. If I had any doubts left about computers and their abilities, this course settled them for me.

Upon our return to Edmonton, I immediately bought some books on computer programming, and the necessary computer equipment; then, I started to design simple programs for estimating electrical work. I soon discovered that my computer programs were most effective if I kept the inputting of data to a minimum, and computer number crunching to a maximum.

I also used my computer programs during the teaching of my estimating courses. I wanted my students to appreciate the benefit of and the simplicity involved in using computer programs for their estimating tasks.

In the meantime, inflation was skyrocketing, and

the Arabs enriched themselves with outrageously high-priced oil. The Canadian people were looking to Alberta for help with cheaper oil supplies, but Alberta Premier Peter Lougheed only managed to anger them with his inflexible oil policy.

On the political front, the Canadian Prime Minister Pierre Elliot Trudeau kicked things off during the October Crisis of 1970. The *Front de liberation du Québec* (FLQ) kidnapped British Trade Consul James Cross on October 5, 1970, and, five days later, the terrorists kidnapped Quebec Labor Minister Pierre Laporte, whom they murdered on October 17, 1970. The prime minister responded by invoking the *War Measures Act*, giving government sweeping powers without trial. However, the government agreed to fly five of the terrorists to Cuba in exchange for James Cross's life. Nevertheless, a few years later, the government jailed these five terrorists after they returned to Canada.

Then, in 1972, the US Watergate scandal occurred, due to a break-in at the Democratic National Committee headquarters at the Watergate office complex in Washington, DC. President Richard Nixon's administration attempted to cover up its involvement in the break-in. However, in 1973, evidence mounted against the president's staff, and eventually against the president as well. This led to the president's resignation on August 9, 1974 – the only resignation of a US president. Fortunately, Nixon's successor, President Gerald Ford, pardoned Nixon, for which he, too, received some criticism.

On September 9, 1976, Mao Zedong, the leader

of the Chinese Communist Party, died. To his credit, he unified China, he improved the status of women, and he stressed China's self-reliance. However, during his reign, his policies caused the death of millions of people, more deaths than for which any other twentieth-century leader had been responsible. His detractors also claim that his policies, especially the Great Leap Forward and the Cultural Revolution, were impediments to industrialization and modernization. Nevertheless, millions of Chinese people sincerely mourned his death.

In 1979, the British people elected Baroness Margaret Thatcher as their prime minister. She was the first woman the British people elected, as well as the longest serving prime minister of Great Britain. She eventually earned the dubbing *The Iron Lady*, after introducing some tough economic measures, and due to her tough stance in the Falklands War.

Also in 1979, a group of Iranian Islamist students took 52 Americans hostage for 444 days, from November 4, 1979, to January 20, 1981, at the American Embassy in Tehran. US President Jimmy Carter called the hostages "victims of terrorism and anarchy." The event reached a climax when the US military attempted the rescue Operation Eagle Claw on April 24, 1980, which failed. Political analysts described the crisis as the "pivotal episode" in the history of Iran-US relations. Some analysts also believe that the crisis was a major reason for Jimmy Carter's defeat in the November 1980 presidential election. Certainly, the Ayatollah Khomeini, who had reasserted himself in Iran, did nothing to help the political situation.

Then, in 1982, Leonid Brezhnev died, and within three years, in 1985, the Soviet Union's Politburo elected Mikhail Gorbachev as the General Secretary of the Communist Party and the Soviet Union. Gorbachev created an atmosphere of open criticism of the communist regime. Consequently, several Soviet Socialist Republics began resisting central control, and democratization increased, thus weakening the central government. Gorbachev tried to draw up a new treaty of union, which would have created a voluntary federation. However, more radical reformists, like Russian SFSR President Boris Yeltsin, favored a faster transition to a market economy, and were happy to contemplate the disintegration of the Soviet Union. The Soviet Union finally collapsed in 1991, when Boris Yeltsin seized power after a failed coup that had attempted to topple Mikhail Gorbachev.

Major transformations in my life continued into the 1980s. In some respects, these were years of sadness. I was coping with the loss of some good friends, and more were disappearing on me during these years. In addition, Vic Webb decided to sell Progress Electric Ltd. to a multinational company from Quebec, for whom I continued working under a contract, which turned out to be a nightmare. Furthermore, I realized that most things were not what they appeared to be, and some things were not what they were supposed to be, while other things were not even what they were defined to be. It took me some time to come to grips with these situations in this world of pretense.

Unfair Negotiations

Most negotiators try to be as fair as possible, but some negotiators use unfairness to gain a clear advantage. My negotiations in Saudi Arabia come to mind. In the late 1970s, I was a member of a Canadian group that wanted to negotiate a partnership with a Saudi Arabian group to finish some incomplete construction projects.

The day of our arrival in Saudi Arabia consisted of handshakes, warm welcomes, a large dinner spread by our hosts, and pleasant conversations. On the second day, the Saudis outlined their partnership conditions for us. We had expected to grant them a 25% partnership, since construction, project financing, and equipment supply would be our responsibility. To our surprise, they demanded 50%. We asked them how they arrived at this figure. They assured us that they had high connections in Saudi Arabia, which would guarantee us receiving some of these projects. I mentioned to them that construction is not always profitable, and I wanted to know if they would share in the losses, if any. Their answer was a resounding "NO!" They explained that we, not they, were in control of construction, and, therefore, responsible for any losses. We thanked them for outlining their partnership conditions to us and went for lunch.

Over lunch, my two companions pointed out that the Saudis' conditions may be acceptable if these construction projects were as lucrative as they are implying. I had misgivings and wanted to see some construction sites.

After lunch, we hired a taxi to take us to various construction sites. Most construction looked abandoned, although the construction equipment was still present. We stopped at one site that showed some activity and talked to the project manager, an English civil engineer. He told us that inflation in Saudi Arabia was running rampant, and skilled labor was almost nonexistent. He added that the productivity was about half what they had estimated. I asked him some questions about the abandoned sites. He said most contractors were bankrupt before they half finished their projects, and the Saudis do not allow construction companies to remove and export their construction equipment. Furthermore, the Saudis do not allow any finance charges. I had heard enough.

Our Saudi group hosted another dinner, but we refused to discuss business. We met with them the next day to ask them a few more questions. Then we thanked them for the information they gave us and for their hospitality. We told them that we would take things under advisement and get back to them in due time. However, we eventually abandoned any further partnership talks, when our Canadian sponsors became disinterested.

My management career in the construction business required me to negotiate every day, sometimes for millions of dollars. These negotiations took a lot of contemplation. Negotiations depend, largely, on what each party has to offer, and on how much influence each party has and wants to use. I never liked using influence unfairly. I believe that what goes around comes around – it is a long road without a bend. For example, if workers make unreasonable demands and go on strike to get them, they may eventually find themselves unemployed.

Think about this type of negotiation. It is similar to needing something badly, like food, and being unable to buy it.

I still remember one unfair negotiation tactic that cost my company dearly. We were negotiating a new contract with the union, and we were requesting some changes to overtime provisions, which the union refused to give us. However, instead of negotiating the issue, the union cancelled contract provisions that were still in effect at the time. They used this tactic to get us to back off. The union's cancellation tactic affected several contractors, and it forced us withdraw our request to keep our contractors' losses to a minimum. We were all wondering what had happened to fair negotiations.

Fortunately, a new union leader took over, and we were once again able to engage in thoughtful and fair negotiations. What I mean by thoughtful negotiations is that each side gave a lot of thought to the needs of the other side, and we tried to solve our mutual problems together. We did not use confrontational practices anymore, and this resulted in new agreements both sides were proud to conclude.

Business negotiations vary from union-management negotiations, because confrontations are less likely to influence the outcome. Nevertheless, business negotiations can still be one-sided.

One negotiation comes to mind. I conducted it with the owners' representative of an industrial project. The owners had delayed our work with new designs in many areas, and, at the completion of the project, we submitted a compensation claim for $5.5 million to cover our production losses. The owners accepted some responsibility for our cost overruns, but offered to pay us only 20% of our claim.

I requested a face-to-face meeting with the owners' representative, and asked him how the owners had arrived at their offer. He gave me a long explanation and a formula that they had used, which excluded their estimated production losses accountable by us. I promised him to consider it and requested a further meeting with him a week hence. He agreed.

Back at my office, I rigorously applied his formula to our contract breakdown, and came up with $3.5 million. Then, I contacted the president of our company and explained to him why we were unlikely to receive $5.5 million, but that we may be able to convince the owners to pay us $3.5 million.

Our president had no problem accepting $3.5 million, but he wanted to know how I planned to convince the owners to pay us that amount, since they had offered us only $1.1 million. I told him that I planned to show the owners' representative that his own formula comes up with $3.5 million, and reason with him to pay us that amount. He said, "Go ahead and try it."

When I met with the owners' representative the

following week, I showed him my spreadsheet, and explained to him how the formula he gave me came up with $3.5 million. He was genuinely surprised, but could not dispute my figures. He excused himself, left the office, and took my spreadsheet along. When he returned after about half an hour, he said that the maximum he could offer me is $2.8 million. I phoned our president and relayed the owners' new offer to him. "Take it!" he said.

This sort of negotiation is still one-sided, because possession is truly nine points of the law. The owners knew that if we were to proceed to trial we would probably spend a million dollars in legal fees, without any assurance we could convince a judge that the amount of our claim is valid.

Nevertheless, my success in getting the owners to up their original offer of $1.1 million to $2.8 million was entirely due to a thoughtful process of negotiation. I used no confrontational tactics, like threatening them to go to trial. I kept in mind that the amount of a construction-delay claim is usually subjective and biased, and if the claim recipient shows such bias to a court, the claimant might receive even less. Besides, we also had to keep in mind that we wanted to do business again with these owners, and they knew it, too. So, have the owners used their power unfairly? Perhaps, but, from their viewpoint, the amount of the claim was unsubstantiated, even after seeing accurate records of production by the contractor.

Arabian Culture Shocks

I received my first Arabian shock when I obtained my Saudi Arabian visa for the trip I mentioned in the previous section. The Saudis stamped the visa right into my passport. It had a condition that if I planned a stopover in Israel, either before or after my visit to Saudi Arabia, this would invalidate the visa. I had actually toyed with the idea of a stopover in Israel, but, with this visa provision, I quickly abandoned the notion.

My second Arabian shock came when I arrived at the airport in Saudi Arabia with my two companions. A half dozen Saudis were pointing submachine guns at us while we were standing in line, waiting for clearance by the Saudi customs officials. A sign on the wall warned us not to take pictures of the airport, or any government or military facilities. We found out later that the Saudis arrested an English civil engineer for spying. All he did was take a picture of the harbor when he saw the fin of a shark. He spent six months in a Saudi jail before the British government could get him released.

When we checked in at our hotel, the hotel staff also warned us not to take pictures of Saudi women. I am not even sure we saw any Saudi women on this trip. What we saw were some figures covered in burkas. A burka is a large, pitch-black piece of cloth draped over the body from the top of the head right to the ground. It covers even the eyes. The sight is eerie.

We assumed these figures were women, but we had no way to ascertain this. In short, we only saw three uncovered women in Saudi Arabia: A homely, uncovered maid of our hosts, in her forties, served us tea. Our hosts did not introduce her to us, and she could have been a foreign worker. We also saw two English women shopping in the souk. We were so pleasantly surprised to see these two uncovered, smiling women that we almost hugged them. They were like a ray of sunshine coming through darkest clouds.

I received my next Arabian shock when I went shopping for a Koran. Our driver took me to three bookstores before he found one that had a translated Koran. The owner of the bookstore wanted seventy-five riyals, and I offered him sixty riyals. We finally agreed on sixty-five riyals, and he put the Koran in a brown paper bag. Then, I felt ashamed, haggling over the price of their sacred book, and put seventy-five riyals on his counter. He immediately started screaming, and yelled something in Arabic. I got scared, grabbed the paper bag, and walked out. When our driver joined me two minutes later, he gave me ten riyals. I asked him why the bookstore owner had made such a fuss. He said that the owner could not have accepted the extra ten riyals after agreeing to a price of sixty-five riyals, because that would be the equivalent of stealing from me, for which he could lose his right hand. I was flabbergasted.

Shortly thereafter, I noticed a Saudi father giving his son a slap on the head. The boy had just picked up a coin from the street. The father gave him a stern lecture, and the boy tossed the coin back to the street. I asked our driver why the boy did not keep the coin. The driver told us that the owner of the coin could claim that the boy stole it from him, and the boy would probably lose his right hand because of this. Again, I was flabbergasted. On the other hand, later, when we were having lunch at our hotel, I picked up a booklet of matches advertising the hotel and quickly put it back, afraid if I kept it, I might lose my right hand. In North America, we have no compunction picking something up that does not belong to us, as long as nobody can accuse us of stealing it.

Another shock came at our last visit with our hosts. They had placed a portable bar in the corner of a huge living room, pointing to it to help ourselves. There must have been a dozen alcoholic beverages on it. My companions gladly complied, but I hesitated. It is illegal to import alcoholic beverages into Saudi Arabia, because of their religion, and I was surprised that our hosts ignored this law to please their guests. Furthermore, I felt uncomfortable breaking a law in a foreign country, even though my own religion accepted the practice of consuming alcohol. Therefore, I stayed seated on the sofa. A few minutes went by, and suddenly a servant put a cup of tea on the table in front of me.

I had a few more shocks before leaving Saudi Arabia. The airline wanted my passport two days before departure. This made me feel insecure in a strange land. I mentioned this to our hosts, and they just laughed. "That's why we travel with two passports," they told me. I wondered if it were possible in Canada to obtain two passports with two Saudi Arabian visas.

I had booked my flight with Lufthansa, and their advice was to come to the airport no later than eight hours prior to scheduled departure, which was 2:00 a.m. in the morning. This meant I had to show up no later than 6:00 p.m. on the prior evening. I thought they were joking, but decided to comply. My compliance turned out to be fortunate. In the first line-up to get my boarding pass, we were required to open our luggage on the floor for the Saudis' inspection. It seemed like opened luggage filled the entire airport. There must have been more than a hundred people in front of me.

My brown paper bag with the Koran in it prominently protruded from the top right corner of my luggage. The book, published in Beirut, Lebanon, was almost four inches thick. However, the Saudi who poked around in my suitcase paid no attention to the brown bag, which could also have contained drugs. This neglect turned out to be a blessing in disguise. I later learned that translations of the Koran are taboo in Saudi Arabia, and my Koran not only had translations in it, but commentaries as well. A Bechtel manager, whom I met on the plane, told me that this Koran could have landed me in a Saudi jail.[1]

It took four hours to get my boarding pass, and, at

---

[1] Upon my return to Canada, an East-Indian friend of mine, who was married to a woman of Islamic faith, offered me $500.00 for the book, because he wanted to understand his wife's religion better. However, I considered my experience acquiring the book a good omen, and refused to part with it.

10:00 p.m., I joined another queue to get my passport back. When I saw the stacks of passports behind the agent's window, I was concerned if they would ever find mine before take-off. However, two hours later, at midnight, I held it in my hand and felt more secure again.

The next line-up was for the Saudi Arabian security check. Again, the Saudis trained their submachine guns on us. The checking process took about an hour, and I walked out to the airfield shortly after 1:00 a.m. What I did not expect was a second security check, this time by the Germans. Lufthansa had set up a row of plywood sheets on sawhorses, and required us to open our luggage and spread the contents out on this makeshift plywood table. The airline's staff inspected the contents carefully, and told us to pack them up again. I finally took my seat in the plane about five minutes before 2:00 a.m. I was almost certain there would be a take-off delay. However, with due speed and dependability, Lufthansa took off at 2:00 a.m. sharp.

We stopped briefly in Athens, Greece, to take on some passengers, but Lufthansa did not allow us to get off the plane. Thus, I can honestly assert that I have been in Athens once, but I never set foot in the city. When we arrived in Frankfurt, Germany, it took only a few minutes for German customs to clear me, with my Canadian passport, and I had the distinct feeling that I was back in the civilized world.

My Artistic Impulses

During my years of contemplation, I also had some artistic impulses. I call them "impulses" because they were inclinations that came and went. For example, I sketched some pencil drawings in my earlier years, but the penchant did not last long. The pencil drawings were acceptable, but my interests turned to other fields. One of these fields was expressing my thoughts in poetic forms. I found this expression more concise and more pleasing.

My poetic impulses started at Christmas 1971. I was temporarily blinded at the time from an explosion in an electrical manhole, and while I was sitting in our living room, listening to Christmas music, and contemplating the meaning of life, generally feeling sorry for myself, a seventy-two-line poem came to me out of the blue. I quickly dictated it to my wife, Renate, because of my blindness. This first poem was one of the few poems that came to me in the German language, which created a translation problem for me. I made several attempts at translation into English, but none of them satisfied me. Finally, I decided to restate the poem rather than to translate it.[2]

My poetic impulses lasted for about twenty years, and then vanished. I would wake up in the middle of the night with a new poem in my mind, and quickly turn on the light and make a note of it before it left me.

---

[2] Since this poem did not end up in my poem book, I have offered it to my readers in my book *Characters* (see the Floyd Brackett chapter).

Similarly, while driving, I would pull over to the roadside when a new poem came to me, and enter it in a small notebook. I had found out that if I did not quickly jot down a new poem when it came to me, I would lose it. Try as I might, I could never completely remember a lost poem.

Eventually, I had a file folder full of typed up poems. However, they stayed in the file folder for a few years. Then I met a woman friend of mine at a funeral. I had given her the odd copy of my poems, and she wanted to know why I do not publish them. I told her the thought had not occurred to me. She asked me to consider it and send her a copy of the book when I decide to publish it. I promised her to do so.

Then came the hard part: I had to retype the poems into my computer. Then, I organized them under plausible headings: Birth, Life, Love, Beauty, Freedom, Enigma, Death, and Continuum. I also created an appendix with poem excerpts and a poem list. Next, I designed my book covers (Renate offered to paint a color background). In my preface, *My Thoughts*, I tried to explain some notions that may have gone through my mind during my poetic impulses. Here is the first paragraph:

> Life is full of enigmas, and millions upon millions of books have been written trying to explain them. Each of the books has achieved a small degree of success – some more than others. The degree depends upon the flow of the mind. As is so often the case in life, the door to baffling situations cannot be forced open. Only with rare,

mental receptiveness can a few glimpses of the enigmas be obtained, and then only briefly – sometimes just for split seconds – and darkness takes over again. There are keys which can help one in such situations; one of them is simplicity.

I finally published my book of selected poems in 1999. My readers liked most of the poems, but some of the poems did not make sense to them, or to me. Perhaps another paragraph of the preface may explain my thoughts when I wrote the poems:

> I sit sometimes contemplating life around me, and I see little that makes any sense, other than improving the physical and mental comfort. Even when I see half-hearted attempts at improving the spiritual life, it seems to me that it is only another way of improving the physical. Therefore, I conclude that people, by and large, have difficulty with this enigma. Perhaps they think it is too difficult to figure out or to accomplish, or that it is just that: an enigma, best left alone. They fail to realize the simplicity of it all, and it saddens me. I could go on in this vein, but enough said.

Well, those were my years of poetic impulses. I also had an appreciation for paintings and sculptures during these years. I still remember an abstract painting I picked up at an auction sale and hung in my living room. My Uncle Adolf, who also proclaimed to be a painter, was always awed when he looked at it.

"What does it mean?" he would ask me. "It portrays the soul of man," I would assure him. He just shook his head.

Inspiring Books

What I mean by "Inspiring Books" are books that impart wisdom. Such books can aid contemplations greatly. I must have read over 1,500 books so far, but only a few were truly inspiring. I liked Bertrand Russell's books, especially his inspiring ones. I also liked Albert Schweitzer's and Albert Einstein's books – the inspiring ones – and I found most of Henry Miller's books inspiring. Henry Miller was one of the most open and honest authors of the twentieth century. Here are some examples, excerpts from Henry Miller's book *A Devil in Paradise*:

> "The one thing about this universe of ours which intrigues me, which makes me realize that it *is* divine and beyond all knowing, is that it lends itself so easily to any and all interpretations. Everything we formulate about it is correct and incorrect at the same time. It includes our truths and our errors. And, whatever we think about the universe in no way alters it. . . .
> "Most of the ills we suffer from are directly traceable to our own behavior. Man is not suffering from the ravages wrought by earthquakes and volcanoes, by tornadoes and tidal waves; he is suffering from his own

misdeeds, his own foolishness, his own ignorance and disregard of natural laws. Man can eliminate war, can eliminate disease, can eliminate old age and probably death too. He need not live in poverty, vice, ignorance, in rivalry and competition. All these conditions are within his province, within his power, to alter. But he can never alter them as long as he is concerned solely with his own individual fate."

Do you find these excerpts inspiring? I do. Some parts of Will and Ariel Durant's books are also inspiring. Here is an excerpt from their book *The Lessons of History*:

"Consider education not as the painful accumulation of fact and dates and reigns, nor merely the necessary preparation of the individual to earn his keep in the world, but as the transmission of our mental, moral, technical, and aesthetic heritage as fully as possible to as many as possible, for the enlargement of man's understanding, control, embellishment, and enjoyment of life."

Do you find this excerpt inspiring? I do. I also find many parts of the Bible inspiring. Here are a few examples I find inspiring:

He that plows his land shall have plenty of bread: but he that follows after vain persons shall have poverty enough. (Proverbs 28:19)

He that is slow to wrath is of great understanding:
but he that is hasty of spirit exalts folly. (Proverbs
14:29)
He that troubles his own house shall inherit the
wind: and the fool shall be servant to the wise of
heart. (Proverbs 11:29)

I find biographies, especially autobiographies, most
inspiring. I also read in dictionaries occasionally, and,
not surprising, I find many inspiring words in them. In
any case, many of the books I have read helped me to
contemplate life. This was a big benefit to me.

My books are definitely the result of my
contemplations. I like my books not because of my
vanity but because they reflect my thoughts, overall
and at any given point in time. One's thoughts, honest
thoughts I mean, are not easy to put on paper at the
best of times. When I wrote my own books, I tried to
make them both interesting and inspiring for my
readers. I tried, as much as possible, to inject my own
experiences, and, if not experiences, some rational
thoughts into these books. I have not yet made a
serious effort to market my books, therefore, I do not
know if they would create a demand. Nevertheless,
they inspired me when I wrote them, and, I hope, they
will eventually inspire my grandchildren. If they do, I
shall consider it a bonus.

I also intended to leave a personal, written record
for my children and grandchildren. I missed such a
written record of my parents and grandparents.
Establishing an historical record of one's ancestors
without having a personal, written record is nearly

impossible and usually inaccurate. I found this out the hard way. If there is any value to my books, which I hope there is, I intend it mainly for my children, my grandchildren, and my closest friends.

Reflections & Novel Concepts

As I look back on my life, I consider myself fortunate. I came through Hitler's war uninjured, at least physically. The years after the war taught me survival techniques, as did my first years in Canada. Then, I was fortunate to meet and marry Renate. Furthermore, we raised two exceptional daughters together, and, in our seniors' age, we are still able to enjoy our four outstanding grandchildren.

As far as my work was concerned, I was fortunate, too. After I served my apprenticeships, I have always been able to do, workwise I mean, what I wanted to do. This made working not just a necessity to earn a living, but also a pleasure. Furthermore, I was very fortunate to work for worthy bosses, and to work with first-rate coworkers. In addition, I was fortunate to have many friends. I value my friends, far beyond any material objects. Talking about material objects, I have always considered them as something loaned to me. In the end, I must return them – even my body and my mind.

My life of contemplation was a little more topsy-turvy, mainly because I have always had more questions than answers – still do. When curiosities are not satisfied, they keep pressing for answers. The enquiring mind seeks satisfactory answers to concepts like God, Satan, angels, heaven, hell, the soul, ghosts, reincarnations, virgin births, the creation of life, and a host of other so-called miracles. Faith in a religion may provide some answers to most people, but science demands proof. Therefore, the curiosity of the scientific mind searches for better answers than any religion provides. In addition, anyone who grew up with a religion must wonder about the various religious differences in the world, and question the value of so many different religions, as well as the differing answers they provide to critical questions.

I am still puzzled, as are many scientists, about the creation of life. No doubt, our scientists will eventually resolve this question to their satisfaction, but it is still nagging my mind. The other big question, whether or not God exists, I think I have resolved, at least to my satisfaction: I am a firm believer in the cause-and-effect concept. Causes often hide themselves, but we can sure see their effects. This is also true with our universal laws. These laws cause everything in the universe to happen – good or bad. Without these laws, or any of them, our universe would not be what it is. Furthermore, we cannot change these laws, even slightly, to accommodate anyone of us. Call these laws what you will, some people call them God, but there is no doubt that they are the Supreme Existence in our universe. This, to my mind, settles the question regarding the existence of God.

PS: I Love You!

In our world, where through natural laws living beings kill and/or eat each other, is there any purpose more meaningful than that? Some people may say, "Yes, prepare for a life hereafter." However, if there is no life hereafter, we should prepare to live our life on Earth with the least amount of friction. One way to accomplish this is to eliminate feelings of hate as much as possible. Feelings of love may not always replace feelings of hate, but eliminating feelings of hate it is a good start. The next step is to develop feelings of love as much as possible.

I have already explored this concept in my book *Thoughts in a Maze* (see the chapter *Love Against Hate*), where I pointed out how the magic of love turned an enemy into a friend. With the elimination of hate, and the promulgation of love, our lives will start taking on a more meaningful purpose. PS: I love you!

Cheerio!